T

is for

Tool

Magick

Kitchen Table Magick Series

by
G. Alan Joel

Esoteric School of Shamanism & Magic

Email: *alan@shamanschool.com*
Website: *www.shamanschool.com*

Publisher: Esoteric School of Shamanism and Magic, Inc.

Disclaimer and Legal Notice:
The Esoteric School of Shamanism and Magic has made every effort to ensure, at the time of this writing, that the information contained in this book is as accurate as possible. The publisher and author make no warranties or representation with respect to the completeness, fitness, accuracy, applicability, or appropriateness of this book's contents. This book's information is provided strictly for entertainment and educational purposes. Should you choose to use or apply the ideas provided in this book, you take full responsibility for your own actions. The publisher and author provide no guarantee that your life will improve in any way should you choose to use the information presented in this book. The ability of the information provided in this book to provide self-help and life improvement to the reader is entirely dependent upon the reader. The reader's ability to gain positive results from the information presented in this book is entirely dependent on the amount of time the reader devotes to the application of the material in this book, the willingness of the reader to dedicate time and effort to learning the materials presented in this book, as well as the reader's own belief system, which may help or hinder the reader's ability to benefit from this book's materials. Since each reader differs according to willingness and openness to the information available in this book, the author and publisher cannot guarantee success or improvement for every individual reader. Neither the publisher nor the author assumes responsibility for the reader's actions, or whether the information is used for negative or positive purposes. The information contained in this book is drawn from tribal traditions—both modern and ancient—as well as the author's 30 plus years' experience researching and teaching this material to students. The information in this book is presented as interpreted by the author, and, as such, may or may not be entirely accurate. In no way should the information presented in this book be a substitute for advice from health or mental health professionals. The author and publisher are not liable—or in any way responsible—for actions

[this page intentionally left blank]

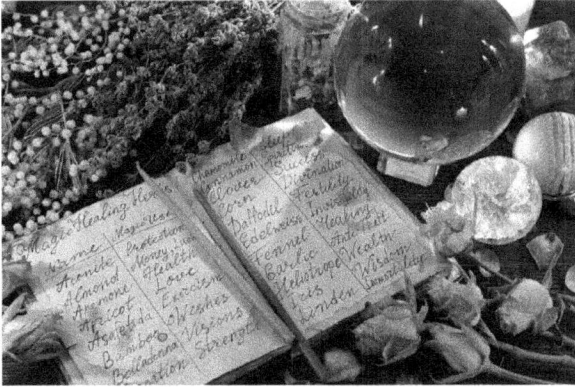

Tool Magick Blessing

Child of Wonder,
Child of Flame
Nourish Our Spirits and
Protect Our Aim.

Magickal beings we all be,
This be true, whether or no we can see.
From creating altars to gathering herbs,
We can all use magickal tools, with great verve!

From blessing our homes to clearing energy,
The Firebowl and Chalice are the tools that we need.
Keying magickal tools is a special technique
That makes the tools ours, and magickally unique.

Beyond Firebowl and Chalice are yet more tools,
Made from everyday objects, how magickal and how cool!
From an apple to paper clips, or some rocks on the ground,
We create magickal tools that work, yet are so simple and
sound.

Thus my will, so mote it be!

Free Gift

To thank you for purchasing this book, I'd like to give you a

100% FREE GIFT

Learn more about your free magickal gift.

Access Your Free Gift at
www.shamanschool.com

Find a complete list of magickal resources on https://amzn.to/3swxvPo. These resources are constantly updated so check back often!

Kitchen Table Tool Magick
Table of Contents

Introduction to Kitchen Table Tool Magick

"We're asking you to trust in the Well-being. In optimism there is magic."
~ Abraham

A Note About This Introduction

This book is one of a series of books in the Kitchen Table Magick series. Each book in the series addresses a specific area of magick (love, money, psychic development, etc.), and is written in a simple "recipe" format for people who want to use magick in their lives immediately. The Kitchen Table Magick series is akin to a Julia Childs recipe book, only these books contain magickal recipes for people to cook up some miraculous and magickal manifestations in their lives.

Because this series was designed so that each person could pick and choose to read just the books that pertain to their current life situation, each book is meant to be readable as a stand-alone book. To introduce the new reader to the series, this introduction to the series is repeated at the beginning of each book. If you have already read one or more books in this series, please feel free to jump ahead to the recipes that interest you. At the same time, some people feel that reviewing the introduction, as well as the "Rules and

Tips," is helpful before diving in. In magickal circles, your will is the guideline so choose whichever route best suits you... the Universe and magickal beings will follow!

What is Magick?

Many people have multiple different ideas about what magick is or can be. For the sake of clarity, here is what we know about magick after more than 35 years of study and practice. Magick is a precision science! It is also:

- The science of deliberate creation.
- The science of effective prayer.
- The science of manifesting Higher Will (substitute whatever Higher Force is most familiar to you) on the energetic and material planes.
- The science of heightened awareness, selective perception, and dynamic, harmonious relationships.
- The study of intention (as per Aleister Crowley, one of the greatest magickal practitioners in history).
- The system of creation, not coercion. Note: The word manipulation is often used in conjunction with magick, but manipulation simply means the use of the hands. It should be an "OK" word without a lot of charge, but currently it is used mostly to mean coercion. Look it up!
- The principle that every intentional act is a magickal act! Magick gives us the ability to communicate with beings on all levels, and allows us to understand, through direct experience, the actual workings of the Universe.
- The traditional path of spiritual growth.
- Not extraordinary knowledge. It is the "normal" way of life. We've just lost access to it. When you have this kind of knowledge in your understanding, you have the ability to resolve spiritual questions that otherwise become catechism. From a magickal point of view, catechism is not acceptable, since a practitioner must experience and verify everything for him or herself. It

avoids the trap of dogma. In past times, having a magickal foundation was essential so that we could talk directly to higher beings in the Universal hierarchy.

- Necessary to effective religious practice.

There is some confusion as to how to spell the word "magick." There are three different commonly used spellings: magick, magic, and majick. Eliphas Levi first used the form "magick" to differentiate religious or ceremonial from stage magick. All forms of spelling are acceptable in what this author teaches.

"I love Kitchen Table Magick! It's the best mix of both mystical and down-to-earth magick I have ever encountered. The fact that I can use items from my pantry is so handy and fun! It literally is about cooking up magic at my kitchen table, and having love show up in the least expected places!"
~ Wendy J., Skokie, IL

Is Magick Real?

Yes. Magick is very real and has existed as a precise science for thousands of years. Whether you use the word magick or another name, this spiritual practice is very real. Every single person can learn to do magick. We are ALL born with the talents and abilities that empower us to do magick. The only reason that magick seems so, well, magickal is that this society no longer teaches the art and science of magick. In the distant past, magickal study was just as important as math, science, or the arts. In fact, magick was and still is the birthright of EVERY planetary citizen.

Can you learn to do the kind of magick portrayed in the movies? Yes... and no. The movies are great at giving you a taste of what you can do with magick, but they are not very accurate. In the Harry Potter movies, for instance, the characters use their Wands for every magickal operation. In reality, you can only use the Wand to handle Air energies. Your Wand would actually explode or catch fire if you tried to use it to throw Firebolts and Fireballs as the characters do in the movie.

So, what can you actually do with magick? Quite a lot. Here is a short list to get you started:

- Balance your energies for healing and manifestation
- Change old beliefs
- Defend yourself against physical and psychic attack
- Heal yourself and others
- Find hidden information and see possible futures (and change the future if you do not like the probable futures you divine)
- Psychically communicate with other beings
- Create sacred space
- Find lost people and objects
- Manifest what you want and need in life

At the very basis of magick is the understanding of the four elements: Air, Fire, Water, and Earth. Called elemental magick, these foundational elements are real. Air, Fire, Water, and Earth are part of our natural everyday environment. What makes them magickal is the understanding of how they operate not just on the physical level, but also at the levels of Mind and Spirit.

For instance, while on the physical level, Air is just the stuff we breathe. On the magickal levels Air is the conduit of psychic communication, enlightenment, understanding, dreaming, and more. If you want more of these things in your life, then you need more magickal Air. How do you get more magickal Air? Wear more Air colors, including white for communication and sky blue for enlightenment and understanding. To take this one step further, you could also use various magickal techniques to take on more Air to make your body lighter. Take on enough Air and you'll be able to levitate.

By just extending your understanding and use of the

basic ingredients of nature, you are doing magick! Seen in this light, magick isn't all smoke and mirrors, nor is it the result of Hollywood special effects. Magick is the result of truly understanding and working with the very elements that are all around you.

One final note: Many masters, including Wayne Dyer, have said, "You'll see it when you believe it." The same is true for magick. In other words, the suspension of disbelief and the willingness not to exercise contempt prior to investigation are requirements for magick to be "real." Magick is all around us, and always is, but our ability to perceive and use the forces of magick depends on our willingness to be open. No one else can show it to you, only your direct experience and observation can "prove" or demonstrate to you that magick is real.

[this page intentionally left blank]

What is Kitchen Table Magick?

Kitchen Table Magick is exactly what it sounds like—a series of simple recipes that you can literally "cook up" at your kitchen table using household ingredients from your own pantry and cupboard.

The Kitchen Table Magick books have been created for ordinary people who want to mix up a little magick in their lives without all the fancy rituals, but simply with everyday ingredients that can be found in the kitchen pantry, bathroom medicine cabinet, or even stuffed in the back of the junk drawer.

The goal of these books is to allow anyone with the desire to learn this craft to mix up magick literally at the kitchen table using simple recipes. What goes into a simple recipe?

- Everyday items as ingredients
- Easy to follow instructions that don't require years of training
- Procedures that take less than two hours from start to finish
- Built-in expertise that allows the magick to do the heavy lifting
- Some friendly advice on how you can help your magickal recipe provide the best results
- Oh, and a few little rules and guidelines about magickal practice in this specific arena that will keep you safe and sound, magickally speaking, when you use these recipes

Kitchen Table Magick Equals:
Quick – Effective – Safe – Everyday Use – Ordinary
Affordable Ingredients

Why Use Kitchen Table Magic?
- Everyone can do magick.
- Magick should be simple, effective, and start working right away, else it is not magick.
- Not everyone has the time or resources to enroll in a school.
- People ask us for magickal help in hundreds of emails everyday... Kitchen Table Magick is designed to help these very people.
- Of the many areas of life, most people only seem to need help in one or two areas, so you need only buy those Kitchen Table Magick books that apply to your needs.
- Magick is for the masses, and should be accessible, affordable, and simple to do. This is what our teacher taught us, and this is the legacy we are paying forward as well.
- While there are many more advanced forms of magick, these books are an introduction to that world so that you can dabble, experiment, try things out, see the result, adjust and amend, and generally have fun... just as you would cooking a meal in your kitchen.
- This book is not for the major foodie, but is perfect for the person who needs magickal help right here, right now!

Who Should Use These Recipes?
- You and anyone you know who would like a little more magick and a little less ordinary reality in their lives.
- Anyone who needs help RIGHT now and doesn't have time to fly to India or Sedona to sit at the feet of a guru.

- Anyone who does not have access to anything but a computer for help and guidance.
- Anyone who wants to do magick and then forget it (all while quietly watching the magick "do its thing").
- Anyone who wants affordable, down to earth magick they can do with regular ingredients in the comfort of home.

When to Use Kitchen Table Magic: Anytime...

- You need help.
- You don't want to do all the heavy lifting (leave that to the Angels, Spirit Guides, Animal Totems, and so forth).
- You seem stuck in a rut or corner with no way out.
- You've been struggling with a problem for a long time and need a resolution.
- You don't know what to do but you need to do SOMETHING.
- You'd like to learn how to practice the craft.
- You want to live a more magickal life and stop dealing with ordinary hassles all the time.

How Do We Know These Recipes Work?

- We teach a slew of these recipes in one-day workshops all over the country, via teleconference, and via videoconference. We also email them to people as part of our school's service work, or post them on our blogs and articles library.
- We have used them for over 35 years and still do, every single day – literally tested out at our own kitchen tables for over 35 years (and at thousands of kitchen tables around the world) for a quarter century or more.
- We receive all kinds of stories and testimonials from happy successful students.

Kitchen Table Tool Magick at Work...

Read the following example to discover how Tool Magick works in real life...

Throw Rocks, Not Hands

When life gets tough, it can be tempting to just throw up our hands and give up in despair! Luckily, I learned in magick class that the magickal way to deal with life's issues is to throw away river rocks rather than throwing up my hands!

I learned that I could "connect" any problems in my life with inanimate objects, such as rocks. The whole magickal ritual has become a deep and soothing kind of meditation whenever life throws me a curve ball.

The ritual is so simple. It goes like this. Whenever I have a problem, I write a list of the different aspects of that problem that I want to toss out of my life. For instance, I was having trouble letting go of a relationship, even though the breakup occurred months ago. My mind just could not stop circling around the "woulda, coulda, shoulda" mantra. I kept trying to contact my former partner, even though we agreed that we would be better off having no contact with each other. I knew I needed to move on, but I just could not seem to do that.

The next step in the ritual is to write a list of aspects of the problem that I wanted to toss out of my life. I wrote down items like:

- circular and repeating thoughts about the relationship
- anger over certain disagreements between me and my ex
- regrets over words and actions
- ... and so on (being careful never to attach a rock to a person).

When the list was complete, I grabbed the list and a cloth bag, and then I went to a nearby park that bordered a river. Walking along the river, I chose a rock for each item on my list. I held each rock in my dominant (right) hand and focused intensely the listed item that I wanted to "connect" to the rock. At the same time, I flowed energy down my arm, into my hand, and into the rock. When the rock felt warm or heavy, I knew that the connection had been made. I put the rock into the bag, and continued the process with the next rock as I walked. Even before the process was complete, the walk had become like a meditation, and I felt more peaceful inside.

When every item on my list had been magickally connected to a rock in my bag, I went to the riverbank. With each rock I took out of my bag, I held the rock while saying the disconnect litany. Then I threw the rock as far as I could into the river. As I emptied my bag, I felt a sense of relief, like a burden had been lifted.

After doing the ritual, I still thought about the relationship, but I no longer obsessed about it. I could easily shift my attention to a different topic. As the weeks went by, I stopped thinking about the relationship altogether, except occasionally in passing or in dreams.

I liked the effect of this ritual so much that I started using it for all kinds of problems that popped up in my life. It worked equally well for big and small problems. More importantly, I felt like the ritual was super soothing to my soul... the process itself, not only the result. I am most thankful to have learned how to turn an ordinary rock into a problem-solving tool!

~ Jake A., Grand Forks, ND

A Few Rules and Tips About Kitchen Table Magick

As with any game, the game of life has its own set of rules. Specifically, the spiritual side of life has rules. Play by those rules and you will stay safe and easily attract what you want into your life. Break those rules and all types of unwanted consequences happen.

These "spiritual rules" are ones that have been observed, both in personal spiritual practice and spiritual practice with various associated groups and teachers. These rules universally govern any spiritual practice, and appear to be in effect whether you know them or not. Unlike ethics and morals, which change with culture and time, these spiritual rules appear to have remained the same throughout time, unchanging, like physical and scientific rules.

The rules in the following section are adapted from *Rules of the Road*, as created by George Dew, co-founder of the Church of Seven Arrows. There are two major rules, which are common to most spiritual practices, along with some minor rules that are specific to our form of magickal practice.

Two Major Rules

These two rules will probably sound familiar, as they appear in most major religions and spiritual practices, most probably because they are common-sense and apply not just to spiritual practice, but to life as well.

First Rule: Golden Rule or Law of Karma
This first rule is literally a "golden oldie":

What you do to the environment or to other beings in the environment brings similar effects back to you in your life.

Often recognized as the Golden Rule or the Law of Karma, this rule tops the list because it reminds all spiritual practitioners of potential unwanted "rebound" or side effects. As your spiritual power, focus, and abilities grow, this rule will have an ever-greater impact on your life unless you exercise caution. The Universe responds more strongly and powerfully to those with focus, power, and ability.

Note: As humanity moves further in the Aquarian Age, many spiritual practitioners have seen more effects from this rule occur faster. In the past, effects of this rule that often took lifetimes to manifest now occur in minutes, days, weeks, or months. In this particular time in Earth's history, karma seems to operate under a "pay as you go" system. Simply stated, expect the effects of the Law of Karma to occur quickly.

Second Rule: The Judgment of "Good and Bad" According to the Universe
This second rule adds clarity and detail to the first rule described previously:

If you are unsure whether your acts are "good or bad"-- that is, whether those acts are in keeping with universal laws on this planet—the Universe will reflect its judgment back to you quickly, according to the "pay as you go" Law of Karma.

This law holds as true for individuals as it does for entire communities, states, nations, or other organized groups. If you are still unsure of the feedback you receive from the Universe, check areas such as your level of health, the soundness of social relationships, your prosperity or lack of, sufficiency of various needs in life, and even your "luck" with appliances and machines. If your luck appears to be consistently poor, then you are probably acting contrary to universal governing laws, regardless of your intentions. The Universe cares about what you do more than what you intend.

Additional Detailed Rules

The following rules offer more detailed standards by which to measure your acts or the acts of others to determine whether these acts are in accordance with universal laws.

- Do nothing that will harm another being unless you are willing to suffer similar or greater harm. What the Universe considers "harm" may be different than what you consider harm.
- Do not bind another being unless you are willing to be similarly bound. An example of binding someone is doing acts in attempt to coerce a specific other person to love you. There is no problem with attracting your soul mate into your life, but doing acts that attempt to coerce a specific other person to love you is a type of binding.
- Never use your spiritual abilities in vain, to show off, or to boost your pride. Using your spiritual abilities from a place of pride usually causes the Universe to bring instant backlash into your life.
- If you choose to charge money or barter for using your spiritual abilities in the service of others, avoid charging extremely high prices. Charge prices for using methods comparable to other professionals, such as an attorney or accountant.
- Never use any spiritual word, chant, litany, or similar "device" unless you are confident in your understanding of its methods, intents, and effects.
- When undertaking a major spiritual operation—one that will require significant effort or attempts to create a major effect in the world—use divination to

determine whether you can safely benefit from such an operation, and to discover the obstacles you must overcome. Divination methods such as pendulum readings, channeling, meditation, and question circles (to name a few) can reveal hidden factors of which you may be unaware.

- In any spiritual endeavor, take your time, think it through, and do it right!

The good news is that you can still use these Tools of Magick rituals. The ones we teach in this book won't get you in trouble with the Universe while also allowing you to perfect the use of magickal tools. With enough practice, you'll soon hone in your abilities of incorporating tools like fire bowls and chalices into your magickal rituals.

The Ingredients of Psychic Magick

"It is essential to have good tools, but it is also essential that the tools should be used in the right way."
~ Wallace D. Wattles

Tools of magick can range from the lavishly designed to the mundane. In this book you will learn the requirements of each magickal tool, then you can create several versions: from richly created ones for your altar to an everyday magickal kit that contains effective magickal tools that look like household items. Magickal tools do have immense power if formed and used correctly. In fact, most magickal tools are simply extensions of the self so whereas you can do many of the same procedures with your bare hands, using a magickal tool extends the reach or adds more force. Many magickal tools could serve double duty as ordinary objects -- such as a Chalice that resembles a wine glass or an Athame that looks like a hunting knife -- the difference between an ordinary household object and a magickal tool is the process of "keying." Keying a tool cleans it of any junky or unwanted energies, aligns the energy of the tool correctly so it can be used magickally, and personalizes the tool to your specific energies so others cannot use your magickal tools without your consent. Besides keying your tools, it is also important to store them correctly.

There is a special tool for each of the 4 elements that conducts the energies of that element. The Air element tool is the Wand, the Fire element tool is the Athame, the Water element tool is the Chalice, and the Earth element tool is the Pantacle or Plate. In addition, there are other tools you may find useful such as a pendulum, staff, a scrying bowl, dowsing rods, a talisman or amulet, or the more basic ones that we will include in this ebook - the Firebowl, Sun Candle, and Book of Shadows. We do also have some tips for you on how to turn many ordinary everyday items you can find around your home into magickal tools.

Tools of Magick Appetizer Recipes

Appetizers: Preparing Magickal Tools

Magickal Altar

Gathering Tools

"I really love the process of putting together a magickal altar and gathering supplies to create magickal tools. I love combining colors and scents and shapes in different ways to make this wonderful, personal, and unique sacred space in my home. My altar also gives me a protected space in which to store my magickal tools. I've never felt more 'witchy'!"
~ Kim R., Deming, NM

[this page intentionally left blank]

Magickal Altar

"The earth is my altar, the sky is my dome, mind is my garden, the heart is my home and I'm always at home — yea, I'm always at Om."
~ Eden Ahbez

Time Required: Forty-Five Minutes

There are specifics for each tool on how to store it properly for protecting it and to maintain keying, but it is also important to have a specific place to store your tools. A magickal altar is a great way to have a personalized place to keep all your sacred objects together including your tools. To create a magickal altar, you need to have a physical space that is free of clutter that you can go to. Find an area preferably in your home that can be just for you and clean it up physically and energetically. You can clear out negative energies by doing a 4 element cleansing (you will learn this in later recipes) or smudging or using the Sun Candle directions in this recipe. Set up an altar: which could be a table, a shelf, a box with a cloth over it or whatever else you would like to use. Add in this space any sacred objects such as a feather or interesting rock you found on a walk, candles, or a talisman or symbol that resonates with you, and of course your magickal tools including your Book of Shadows. A Book of Shadows is one of the first things to get when you are beginning a magickal practice as this is the place you will write down spells in detail or magickal procedures such as divinations or healings you perform. It is important to have a record of the details so you will be able to duplicate the procedure in the future, or in some instances be able to take a spell or procedure down when you are done with it, or you are not getting the results you desire and need to make changes. It is also a way to preserve your work for future generations to benefit from if you wish to pass it on and have a place to record information you get from shamanic research or from higher beings. Your Book of Shadows can be as simple as a notebook or as elaborate as a special leather-bound journal with a carved symbol.

Keep your sacred space area and altar clear of dust and make it a special place just for you. Lighting and charging a Sun Candle is a great way to create sacred space in your special area or anywhere. After selecting your space, physically cleaning it up and setting up your altar, use this recipe to energetically clean your space in addition to or in place of a four element cleansing or smudging.

Ingredients
- a bright yellow candle (Sun Candle) that doesn't have any orange overtones and preferably is unscented
- wooden or paper matches
- a sacred space with altar and any materials to set up and establish it
- a Book of Shadows
- a pen or pencil
- knowledge of the cardinal directions or a compass to find them

Recipe Directions

1. Charge or program the candle with the following steps.

2. Stand or sit in the South facing North with the Sun Candle in front of you.

3. Light the candle using wooden or paper matches. (do NOT use a lighter)

4. Wait until the candle flame is steady and tall.

5. Hold your hands slightly above and around the flame, focusing your attention on the candle and flame.

6. Say the charge verse below in a voice of command (a strong, powerful voice):
   "Child of Wonder,
   Child of Flame,
   Nourish My Spirit,
   And Protect My Aim!"

How to Use the Results of Your Recipe

Leave the candle burning for at least 30 minutes (be sure the candle is on a protected surface such as a plate and is not a fire hazard). At the end of 30 minutes or when you feel ready, blow out the flame (don't snuff it). Be sure and record exactly what you have done to create your altar and sacred space in your Book of Shadows and add to it as you add more objects to the altar. Have fun with creating your altar and make it something pleasing to you aesthetically and energetically. You can make it as large or small as you desire and have room for and as simple or elaborate as you choose.

[this page intentionally left blank]

Gathering Tools

"We shape our tools and afterwards our tools shape us."
~ Marshall McLuchan

Time Required: Sixty Minutes

The first magickal tools you will need besides your Sun Candle and Book of Shadows are the Firebowl and the tools for each of the 4 elements – Wand (Air), Athame (Fire), Chalice (Water) and Pantacle (Earth). This recipe will provide instructions for how to make your own Wand and guidelines for selecting your Athame, Chalice and Pantacle (Plate). Later recipes will give you directions for charging and keying your tools.

Ingredients
- bowl to use as Firebowl (see below description)
- fire clay or fine sand

- a fairly straight limb to make your Wand (see below description)
- small knife to peel off bark and carve
- fine sandpaper
- knife to use as Athame (see below description)
- goblet to use as Chalice (see below description)
- plate to use as Pantacle(see below description)

Recipe Directions

1. **Firebowl:** When choosing a Firebowl, look for one that is made of brass, cast-iron, ceramic or a hard hardwood. It should be 4-6 inches in diameter and 4-5 inches deep. It should also be a shape and size that is easily held with one or both hands and light enough to carry in one hand if necessary. Make sure your Firebowl is of a shape that will be stable when placed on a flat surface. The shape of the bowl should also be curved-in and flared back out at the top rim to promote a "columning" of incense or smoke. Fill it with ground fire clay or clean, fine sand. Non-scented cat litter (which is ground clay) works well as long as it does not have chemicals or deodorants in it. Put 1-2 inches in the bottom of your Firebowl as an insulator to protect the Firebowl itself, your hands, and any surfaces from the heat.

2. **Wand:** You can purchase a Wand, but we recommend making your own so that it is more personalized to your own energies. To make your own wand, first select a limb, by taking a walk in an area with trees. Find one that is ¼ to 3/8 inch diameter from a live tree or recently fallen from a live tree, is light-weight and light colored, and is no longer than the bend of your elbow to the tip of your middle finger. (white pine, birch, peeled willow, aspen or yucca-stalk are examples of good Air-oriented woods) Balsa wood, while light, is too soft to use for a Wand. Avoid materials like glass, which has too much water energy, and crystal. Crystal is an infinite-spectrum

material (in terms of the energy it conducts), which makes it very hard to control. If you take the limb from a live tree, be sure to ask permission of the tree first. Your wand is an important magickal tool and should be personal to you so take your time in selecting one that draws you to it. Once you have selected your limb, use a small knife to peel the bark off the limb and use your fine sandpaper to go over the limb and make it smooth to the touch. Then carve a notch at the end of the limb that was closest to the trunk of the tree. Carve a large, open notch in this base end to allow your wand to easily draw in Air energies. The notch will resemble a "V" shape. Now use your knife to whittle a slightly rounded point on the growing end of the limb (opposite end from the notch). This will be the tip of the Wand.

3. **Athame:** In choosing your Athame, you can select anything from a kitchen knife to a hunting knife as long as it is a single-edged, straight blade made of high carbon, nickel alloy or chrome alloy steel, that has a full tang. (steel goes all the way through the handle, or nearly all the way through) Be sure that it is not a folding knife. Pick a knife that you enjoy holding and fits comfortably in your hand. Often hunting knives come with a leather sheath and this is a bonus for storing your Athame.

4. **Chalice:** Select a goblet-shaped drinking cup that has a stem for easy handling and that has a good-sized bowl (you'll want to be able to store small objects in your Chalice). The bowl can have patterns on it as long as the patterns are not too deep. Glass or ceramic work best, although you can also use Chalices made of silver, pewter or copper. It should be made of only one material. Avoid combinations of materials, such as glass and metal. Some people prefer clear glass because you can see what is in the Chalice, and other people prefer Water Blue Chalices since we often use Water Blue in working with the Chalice. Wood

Chalices do not work well because they have too much Air element in them.

5. **Pantacle (Plate):** Select a round plate 6-10 inches in diameter, made of wood, ceramic or porcelain, glass, or metal that is of earth tone colors or has plant based designs in earth tones. Find a round plate that doesn't have deeply carved patterns. You should be able to hold it easily by placing your thumbs in the center and the rest of your fingers on the edge.

How to Use the Results of Your Recipe

In the next recipe you will learn how to charge your Firebowl and Chalice. All your tools will need to be "keyed", but since these two tools are used in the keying process, they also need to be "charged". Charging these two tools programs them for a specific purpose and the charge verse varies depending on what that purpose is. Since we will be programming them to cleanse and key our other tools, we will be giving you the charge verse for this purpose in following recipes.

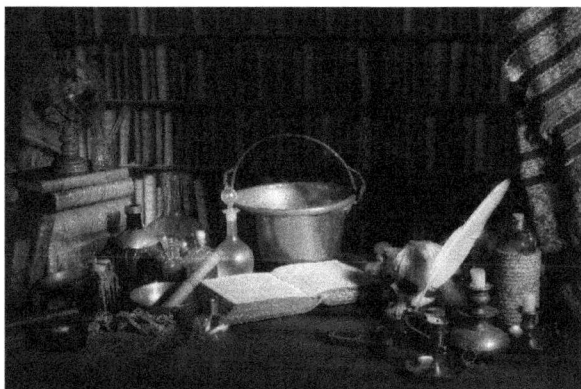

Tools of Magick Main Course Recipes

Main Courses: Cleansing, Keying, and Using Magickal Tools

Charging Firebowl and Chalice

Cleansing and Keying Tools

Using Magick Tools

"Wands are not just for Harry Potter or movie screens. In fact, these courses have taught me how to make all kinds of magickal tools like athames (knives), chalices, pantacles, pendulums... and way more! Amazing, magickal, delightful."
~ Jonas W., Jackson, MS

[this page intentionally left blank]

Charging Firebowl and Chalice

"Any program is only as good as it is useful."
~ Linus Torvalds

Time Required: Sixty Minutes

To cast strong magic spells and perform other magickal procedures correctly, your magick tools need to be clean of junky energies. Your Firebowl is a tool that can cleanse your other magickal tools. It is also used in keying some of your other tools. Charging your Firebowl programs it for a specific purpose which in this case is to cleanse your other magickal tools. Since magick is a precision science, charging your Firebowl for certain operations makes it more effective by stating the intended purpose and programming that into the tool. Charging is not an invocation or prayer to spirit-beings or deities, just a program.

Firebowl

Cleansing a person, space, or object with a Firebowl is called a two-element cleansing since the Firebowl covers the elements of Air and Fire (notice it says "Air and Fire where you are cast" in the charge verse). Firebowl cleansings are good for removing psychic imprints from walls, jewelry, objects, people or just about anything else. Throughout history almost every spiritual, magickal and religious system on Earth has used the Firebowl (sometimes called a "thurible"). While it has primarily been used for cleansing and purification of areas, people, and objects, the Firebowl can also be used as an aid to meditation or divination. This recipe gives you the directions on charging your Firebowl to use it in keying your other tools. The process is similar for charging it to do a house cleaning, cleaning objects or people or other magickal procedures. The charge verse will vary according to the purpose you intend to use it for.

Ingredients
- Sun Yellow candle
- wooden or paper matches
- Firebowl as described in *"Gathering Tools"* recipe
- charcoal disk
- wood shavings
- pine resin
- ground sage

Recipe Directions
1. Light your Sun Yellow candle with wooden or paper matches and charge it by cupping your hands over the flame. Once the flame of the candle is burning tall and bright (called a working flame), say the following litany in a voice of command:
   "Child of Wonder
   Child of Flame
   Nourish My Spirit
   And Protect My Aim"

2. Stand or sit South of your Firebowl facing North with your Firebowl and materials in front of you.

3. Light the charcoal disk with a match that you light with the flame of your Sun Yellow candle. The charcoal will begin sparking within seconds. If the charcoal is old or damp, you may need to use tongs to hold it over the flame for several minutes. Also, with old or damp charcoal, you may want to light the top of it in the center of the bowl-shaped depression so that the materials you put on top will burn more easily. Most of you will realize that once the disk is lit, you don't touch it with your hands, but for beginners who have never used one before we like to add this word of caution – It is hot, just like a charcoal on a BBQ grill. (Be sure to have proper ventilation when you are burning the charcoal.)

4. Once the charcoal is lit in the center of your Firebowl, breathe in Sun Yellow energy from your candle and blow out Sun Yellow energy into the charcoal.

5. Add wood shavings to the charcoal, then pine resin, then sage as needed until the Firebowl is producing a good column of smoke.

6. A voice of command should be used when saying the charge verse. The verse will vary according to what you are programming the Firebowl for. The charge verse for cleansing tools is as follows:
   "Fire and Air where you are cast,
   Let no spell nor adverse purpose last,
   Not in accord with me!
   Cleanse these tools and cleanse their space,
   Far from here send baneful trace!
   Thus my will, so it be!"

How to Use the Results of Your Recipe
The Firebowl does not need to be keyed like other magickal tools do. It keys itself every time you light it. And not all procedures will need a charged Firebowl, but cleansings do and keying your other magickal tools, which you will be learning in recipes that follow, require it.

Chalice
You can charge or program your Chalice for specific purposes, just as you charged your Firebowl. Whereas the Firebowl deals with the elements of Fire and Air, the Chalice deals with the elements of Water and Earth. The charge verses are the same except for the first line. You can charge both keyed and non-keyed Chalices.

Ingredients
- chalice as described in the *"Gathering Tools"* recipe
- pure water (rain, spring or distilled water)
- non-iodized sea salt
- water blue color source (can be square of colored paper a medium blue color - lighter than navy blue)
- knowledge of directions or compass to find them

Recipe Directions
1. Sit in the South facing North. Have your Chalice, pure water, non-iodized sea salt and a Water Blue color source handy.

2. Fill the bowl of the Chalice halfway with pure water (rain, spring or distilled water).

3. Add a pinch of sea salt or crushed rock salt and swirl the water and salt clockwise (to the right).

4. Breathe Water Blue into the water in your Chalice using your color source as a reference, swirling the water clockwise as you breathe.

5. In a voice of command, say the verse below, breathing Water Blue into the Chalice and swirling the water clockwise between each line and after you complete the verse. As with the Firebowl, you may substitute words in the verse depending on your purpose:
   "Water and Earth where you are cast,
   Let no spell nor adverse purpose last,
   Not in accord with me.
   Cleanse these tools and cleanse their space,
   Far from here send baneful trace!
   Thus my will, so it be!"

6. Remember to breathe Water Blue into the Chalice after you finish the last sentence of the verse.

How to Use the Results of Your Recipe

You will need a charged Chalice when you get to the recipe on keying your Plate or Pantacle which is the Earth tool, and you will charge a secondary Chalice to help you key your primary Chalice. You will also use a charged Chalice for doing a four element cleansing in one of the following recipes.

[this page intentionally left blank]

Cleansing and Keying Tools

"The objective of cleaning is not just to clean, but to feel happiness living within that environment."
~ Marie Kondo

Time Required: Sixty Minutes

Before using your magickal tools, they need to be cleansed to remove any junky, unwanted, or negative type energies and they need to be keyed to personalize them to yourself and align the molecules so that energy flows in the proper direction. Your tools each need to be stored in a particular facing direction and in a particular way to keep them cleansed, keyed and in good working order. This recipe will give you the instructions to do this for each tool.

Ingredients
Wand
- wand as described in "Gathering Tools" recipe
- knowledge of directions or compass to find them

- charged Firebowl producing smoke as described in "Charging Firebowl and Chalice" recipe
- piece of natural fiber material such as cotton, wool, leather or silk (no synthetic materials) large enough to wrap around Wand for storing

Athame

- athame as described in "Gathering Tools" recipe
- sun candle
- wooden or paper matches
- knowledge of directions or compass to find them
- charged Firebowl producing smoke as described in "Charging Firebowl and Chalice" recipe
- sturdy magnet or lodestone at least ½ inch wide
- sheath that came with knife or piece of natural fiber material such as cotton, wool, leather or silk (no synthetic materials) large enough to wrap around Athame for storing

Chalice

- two charged chalices as described in the "Gathering Tools" and "Charging Firebowl and Chalice" recipe
- charged Firebowl producing smoke as described in "Charging Firebowl and Chalice" recipe
- spring water
- sea salt
- pure cotton cloth
- piece of natural fiber material such as cotton, wool, leather or silk (no synthetic materials) large enough to wrap around Chalice for storing

Pantacle

- plate as described in the "Gathering Tools" recipe
- charged Firebowl as described in "Charging Firebowl and Chalice" recipe
- charged Chalice as described in "Charging Firebowl and Chalice" recipe
- pure cotton cloth

Wand
Recipe Directions

1. You will now cleanse and "key" your wand to your own energies to make it uniquely your own and to align the molecules in the tool so that the energies flow in a certain direction. To key your wand:

   - First feel the energetic quality of your Wand by running your hands over it or holding it 1-2 inches above your arm and sweeping it up and down. Remember how your Wand feels before it is keyed.

   - Stand in the South facing North and charge your Firebowl as described in the previous recipe *"Charging Firebowl and Chalice"*.

   - Once the Firebowl is charged and sending up a thick column of smoke, hold your Wand in the middle of the smoke column with the tip pointing North and the base (the notched end) towards you.

   - Start pulling the Wand through the smoke toward you with the notch end entering the smoke first. Hold the Wand an inch above the rim of the Firebowl.

   - Keep pulling the Wand slowly and deliberately through the smoke, rolling it a little as you pull it through. Look for the smoke to stick to the Wand.

   - Once the smoke sticks to the entire length of the Wand, hold it vertically in the column of smoke, notch end down, about 1 inch from the charcoal.

   - With your intention, pull the smoke up along the entire length of the Wand until it covers the entire Wand and floats off the tip. This step aligns the molecules in your Wand so that energies move from base to tip only. This protects you from any

39

energies coming back at you.

- Feel your Wand again. It should feel different to you now that it has been keyed. If you do not feel the difference, repeat the process with the Firebowl.

How to Use the Results of Your Recipe

Once you've keyed your Wand, take special steps to store and maintain that keying. Do not drop it, hit it against anything hard, strike it, sand it, or put it in water – all these actions will un-key your Wand. When you're not using your Wand wrap it in natural fiber material such as cotton, wool, leather, or silk (no synthetic materials) and place it on your altar or other magickal storage area lying East to West, with the notched end pointing East. If you don't use your Wand every 2-4 weeks, it will become un-keyed, and you may have to key it again. Key your Wand any time it doesn't seem to be working properly or producing the results you normally get.

Athame
Recipe Directions

1. You will need to key your Athame to align the molecules and make it uniquely yours. Start by sitting in the South facing North.

2. Test the energetic feel of the Athame before keying by running your hands over the tool or running the Athame down and slightly above the surface of your arm. (Since the Athame is a sharp knife, observe safety precautions when working with it. At no time does the sharp edge of blade or tip of blade physically touch your body or anyone else's. It is used to transmit energy and project that energy which can touch, encompass, or surround the body).

3. Charge your Firebowl as per instruction in the

"Charging Firebowl and Chalice" recipe.

4. Once the Firebowl is charged and smoking steadily, hold your Athame by the handle between your thumb and forefinger, tip facing North, handle toward you. The blade of the Athame should be flat and parallel to the ground.

5. Slowly pull the Athame through the smoke toward you, holding it one inch above the Firebowl. The handle should enter the smoke first.

6. Keep pulling the Athame deliberately through the smoke until the smoke begins to stick to the Athame. Then turn the Athame over and smoke the other side of the blade, holding it in the same manner, until the smoke sticks.

7. Hold the Athame vertically in the column of smoke, tip pointing up with handle about one inch over the charcoal. With your intention, pull the smoke up over the tip of the Athame until you see a thin sheath of smoke cover the entire Athame and float off the tip of the blade.

8. Hold the Athame with the tip pointing North, the blade parallel to the ground. Stroke each side of the blade with the magnet from handle to tip, using 3-5 strong, firm strokes. Put your intention into each stroke, since this lines up the molecules in the blade.

9. To lock in the keying, hold the knife vertically (tip pointing up) about 2 to 3 inches above the flame of the Sun Yellow candle. Using your intention, pull the Sun Yellow energy up the Athame from blade base to tip. When you see the flame of the Sun Yellow candle stretch up toward the Athame, the energy has reached the tip of the Athame. You can stop pulling at that

point.

10. To check whether your Athame is keyed, hold it vertically in the column of smoke from the Firebowl again, but don't pull. If the smoke moves vertically up the Athame, then it is keyed. If not, re-key your Athame starting with step 4.

11. Test your Athame by running it above and down your arm again. You should notice an energetic difference.

How to Use the Results of Your Recipe

Once your Athame has been keyed, store it in its sheath if it came with one or in material of a natural fiber such as leather, cotton, silk, or wool. Place it on your altar or other magickal storage area with the handle facing South and the tip facing North. When you use your Athame, take precautions not to bump, hit or grind it or bring it into contact with excessive heat or any kind of magnetic field. These activities will un-key your Athame.

Chalice
Recipe Directions

1. Gather your charged Firebowl, pure water, sea salt, pure cotton cloth, the Chalice you want to key and a spare Chalice (which does not have to be keyed).

2. Feel the energy of your Chalice (the one you want to key) before you begin by sticking your hand into the bowl of the Chalice or holding your palm above the bowl.

3. Cleanse and charge your spare Chalice and the one you want to key as described in the recipe *"Charging Firebowl and Chalice"*.

4. Hold the Chalice you are keying upside down by the stem in the column of smoke from your Firebowl.

Allow the smoke to drift into the bowl of the Chalice for 15-30 seconds. Pull the Chalice away from the smoke and see if the smoke sticks to the inside of the bowl (little streamers of smoke will billow out of the bowl if the smoke is sticking). If not, put the Chalice back over the Firebowl until the smoke sticks.

5. Smoke the outside of your Chalice by holding the Chalice sideways over the smoke with the bowl facing West (or your left), and slowly rotating it toward you. Alternatively, you can point the bowl East, in which case you would slowly rotate the Chalice away from you. Smoke the entire outside of the chalice until smoke sticks everywhere.

6. Fill your spare Chalice with the water and dip one corner of your cotton cloth into the water of your spare Chalice. Use the wet area of the cloth to wipe the inside of the bowl of the Chalice you are keying. Start at the bottom center of the bowl and begin wiping clockwise (imagine a clock in the bottom of the bowl), moving your cloth upward around the bowl in a spiral. Wipe with pressure and intention until the entire inside of the bowl has been wiped.

7. Without stopping, wipe the rim of bowl and then continue wiping the outside of the Chalice in the same direction you have been moving. Do not change directions once you reach the outside – the wiping should be in one smooth continuous stroke. Your cloth should not leave the chalice surface. You may want to have another person watch you to ensure that you do not change directions.

8. When you reach the base, turn the Chalice over and continue to wipe the foot of the Chalice from the outside edge in. If your Chalice has a hollow foot and stem, be sure and wipe all the way up into the stem.

9. Using a dry corner of your cotton cloth, repeat the wiping procedure remembering to wipe with steady pressure and intention.

10. Test the energy of your Chalice again and notice any differences.

How to Use the Results of Your Recipe

When you key your Plate you will be able to store your keyed Chalice standing on your Plate, unwrapped. Until you key your plate, though, you will need to store your Chalice wrapped in a pure, natural material such as cotton, wool, linen, silk, or leather. Once your Chalice has been keyed, avoid hitting the Chalice on hard surfaces since this can un-key it. You can use your Chalice for everyday use, but make sure that if you wash or dry your Chalice, that you use the same wiping motions as you did when you keyed it. This will ensure that you don't un-key your Chalice. Do not wash your Chalice in the dishwasher. If it begins to look tarnished or cloudy from lack of use, re-key it. Your Chalice should stay keyed if stored properly.

Plate
Recipe Directions

1. To begin, gather your charged Firebowl and charged Chalice (see directions in *"Charging Firebowl and Chalice"* recipe) and a pure cotton cloth.

2. Feel the energy of your Plate before you begin by moving your palm back and forth above it.

3. Sit in the South facing North with your charged Firebowl producing smoke as described in *"Charging Firebowl and Chalice"* recipe.

4. Hold your Plate upside down (dished side down) in the column of smoke from the Firebowl. Allow the

smoke to drift onto the Plate for 15-30 seconds. If the Plate has been previously used by other people or for another purpose, it may take more time for the smoke to clear out the energies. Pull the Plate away from the smoke and see if the smoke sticks to it (little streamers of smoke will billow off the Plate if the smoke is sticking). If not, put the Plate back over the Firebowl until the smoke sticks.

5. Smoke the bottom of your Plate in the same way until the smoke sticks.

6. Dip a corner of your cotton cloth into the water of your charged Chalice. Use the wet area of the cloth to wipe the top of the Plate (the concave side). Start at the center of the Plate and begin wiping clockwise, moving your cloth outward in a spiral. Wipe with pressure and intention until the top of the Plate has been wiped.

7. Without stopping or lifting the cotton cloth from the Plate continue wiping by moving to the rim of the Plate, then turn the Plate over and continue wiping the back of the Plate in the same direction. Do not change directions once you reach the back – the wiping should be in one smooth continuous stroke. When you turn the Plate over you will be wiping in a counter-clockwise direction. You may want to have another person watch you to ensure that you do not change directions. If you change directions when you start wiping the back, your Plate may split in half during intense magickal operations. You could end up with two very thin but completely round plates.

8. Using a dry corner of your cotton cloth repeat the wiping procedure remembering to wipe with steady pressure and intention.

9. Test the energy of your Plate again and notice any differences.

How to Use the Results of Your Recipe

Unlike the other tools, your Plate will stay keyed without being wrapped in a natural material. In fact, if you store your Chalice on top of your Plate, the Plate will help maintain the keying of the Chalice. If you will be traveling with your Plate you may want to wrap it to prevent anything from hitting it. Striking, hitting, or dropping your Plate will un-key it. You can use your Plate for everyday use but make sure that if you wash or dry your Plate you use the same wiping motions as you did when you keyed it. This will ensure that you don't un-key it. Do not wash your Plate in the dishwasher.

Using Magick Tools

"Intuition is the number one tool in the toolbox."
~ Matthew Mellon

Time Required: Sixty Minutes

If you have followed the recipes in order throughout this eBook then your magick tools have been selected or made and are now keyed. You are now ready to start using them. There are many procedures that can be done using your tools. Some procedures must be done using tools and others can be done with your bare hands but are stronger or give you a longer reach with tools. In this recipe we will give you one magickal procedure that you can perform for each of the magickal tools we have explored thus far. This will give you some practice using each tool and becoming familiar with it.

Firebowl: Two Element House Cleansing

We have already explored that the Firebowl can be used for cleansing and keying other magickal tools. One of the many other uses for it is doing a two-element (Fire and Air) house cleaning. Firebowl cleansings are good for removing psychic imprints from walls, as well as from jewelry, objects, people or just about anything else. Cleansings cannot banish spirits or beings – only banishments can do that, but cleansings can get rid of the psychic residue left by any beings. It's good to clean sick rooms, objects that belonged to other people or anything or anyone that may have come in contact with any kind of trauma. For instance, if you and a loved one have a severe fight in a room in your house, it's a good idea to cleanse the room and burn the Sun candle to restore sacred space. If you receive a gift from anyone that may have been influenced by other people's energy, clean it with the Firebowl. If you come into contact with people who have health or emotional issues it's good to cleanse yourself. A good magical rule of thumb is, "If in doubt, clean it!" This recipe will give you directions for doing a house cleaning.

Ingredients
- firebowl
- charcoal disk
- wood shavings
- pine resin
- ground sage
- wooden or paper matches
- sun candle

Recipe Directions
1. Charge your Firebowl following the directions given in "Charging Firebowl and Chalice" recipe. You may want to put little containers of extra sage, wood shavings and pine resin in the Firebowl, around the edges, so you can add more materials as needed.

Metal jar lids or tiny sauce dishes work well for this purpose.

2. Carry your Firebowl with you and move to the center of the East-most wall of the area you want to cleanse. If you want to cleanse your entire house, go to the East-most interior wall of the East-most room in your house. If your house has multiple stories, start on the lowest story, and work your way up. If you are cleansing just an area, go to the East-most wall of that area.

3. Facing the wall, move the Firebowl so that the smoke from the bowl creates a Lemniscate on the center of that wall about chest height. A Lemniscate looks like a "Lazy 8" or the infinity symbol (∞). Watch the smoke to make sure it "sticks" to the wall (i.e., doesn't bounce off the wall). If the smoke bounces off, draw another Lemniscate (or several more) until it sticks.

4. Move clockwise or to the right down the wall, holding your Firebowl chest high, allowing the smoke to trail along the wall and blowing the smoke onto the wall if necessary. If the smoke bounces off any section of wall, go over that area again, pushing the smoke into the wall with the action of the Firebowl and with your intention. Keep going over that section until the smoke is absorbed. These areas usually indicate negative psychic or emotional energies.

5. Put a Lemniscate in the middle of each wall, and over mirrors, windows and any shiny or glassy surface (especially black glass). If you're doing an especially large area, you may need to add extra wood shavings, sage, and resin as you go.

6. When you arrive back at your starting point, put a second Lemniscate over your first one to tie it off.

(completes the cleansing)

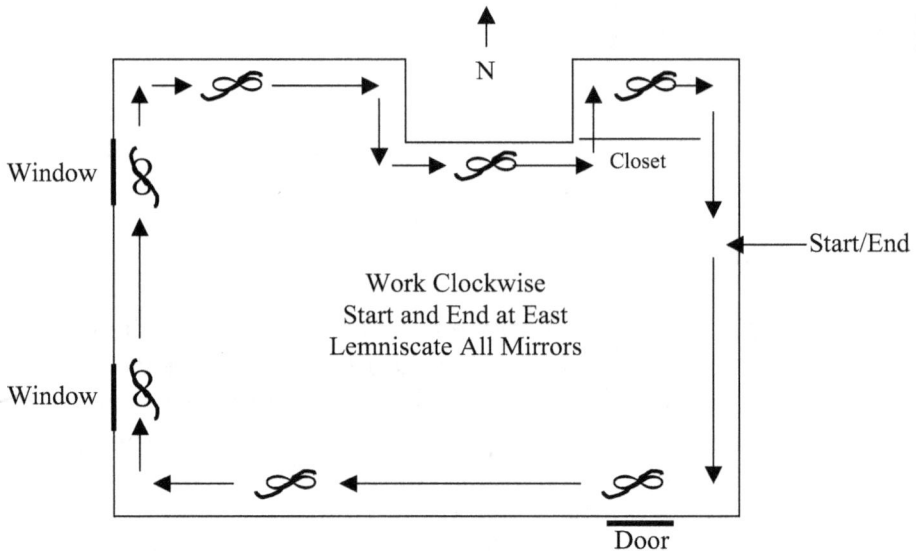

Window

Window

N

Closet

Start/End

Work Clockwise
Start and End at East
Lemniscate All Mirrors

Door

How to Use the Results of Your Recipe

If you are cleansing a large house, you may need extra pieces of charcoal. You can add a new piece of charcoal directly onto the original charcoal without having to recharge the Firebowl. If you want to do a very thorough cleansing, make sure to smoke all cupboards, closets, nooks, crannies, and shelves. Treat walk-in closets as small rooms. Be sure to carefully smoke and Lemniscate all mirrored and glass surfaces. Mirrors and windows are doorways that allow beings to penetrate your shields through the reflection. The black mirror is an access to all worlds. Treat all doors as walls. If you come to an open door, smoke the side of the door closest to you, then go around the back of the door and smoke that. Then move down the wall that is contiguous to the back of the door. If you come to a door that leads outside the house, treat the inside of the door as a wall and don't do the back (outside face) of the door. If you are cleansing an area only, shut all the doors to that area and treat the doors as walls. If you have an opening that has no door, draw a Lemniscate across the center of the open space.

Wand: Sending Wand Messages

You can use your Wand to send a message to another person. This is a great way to help get your point across to someone who you think is not listening to you or to facilitate a communication between yourself and another person by sending a message before you talk to them in person preparing the way or sending a message after your communication reiterating your main points for them to remember. Wand messages act on the mind or consciousness of the recipient and usually appear in the form of a sudden thought.

Ingredients

- a keyed Wand
- white, Clear, and/or Sky Blue color sources (can be squares of colored paper)
- knowledge of direction East or compass to find it

Recipe Directions

1. Decide whether you want to use Clear, White or Sky Blue, and have your color source ready. White or Sky Blue tend to be more effective than clear. White acts on the mind and Sky Blue acts on the spiritual level. If the person is very busy mentally you may want to choose Sky Blue so you won't have to compete with all of the person's White energy. Send your message when the person is likely to be mentally or spiritually available (i.e., not in the middle of a busy meeting).

2. Face East, and hold your Wand in your output hand (hand you naturally point with). Hold the notched end in the hollow of your hand and put your first two fingers and thumb around the Wand. Cock the elbow

of your output hand so it is at a 90 degree angle to the ground, arm extended out from the shoulder so the Wand is pointing straight up.

3. Pull in the Air color you want to use with your input hand, then look at your Wand. Take three breaths and really push the color into your Wand with each breath. The Wand may quiver as you push energy into it.

4. Turn in the direction of your output hand and see the person's face you wish to send a message to beyond your arm.

5. Straighten your arm, palm up and shoot the energies out of the Wand at the "mockup" of the person's face with an outward breath. At the same time, say your message in a voice of command (strong voice). Be sure your palm is up! If you send a message with palm down the energies shoot out of the Wand with laser beam force. This may overwhelm the person with Air energies and make them too distracted or "spaced out" to understand your message. Remember, too, that if you make a person distracted and they get into trouble as a result, the Universe will hold you accountable!

How to Use the Results of Your Recipe

Since Air is a lightweight element, it is a good choice for facilitating communication because it doesn't have much force so you can't command anyone to do anything against their will, which keeps you on the right side of Universal Rules of the Road. You can send an idea but the recipient is still able to decide whether to act on that idea or not. Short messages, like "Call me", or "I love you" seem to work the best with Wand messages. To increase the effectiveness of your message, send it more than once at different times of the day or try sending it in different colors. The person may get the message but not know who sent it or they may get the idea but be too busy to act on it.

Athame: Fire Omnil

This recipe will teach you how to build a Fire element omnil around yourself using your Athame to draw 3 energy circles around yourself. Every circle will be large enough to encompass the height and width of your entire body. The first circle is horizontal (time) and chest high – like a chest-high hula-hoop. The second circle is vertical (space) and directly in front of your body. The third circle is also vertical (events) and is to your side. All 3 circles must be drawn in the order given, drawn at right angles to each other and must all be present for the omnil to work.

Ingredients
- keyed Athame
- color sources for Fire element colors: Sun Yellow, Yellow Orange, Red Orange, Bright Red, Red Purple, and Electric Blue or whichever one of these you choose to use (sources can be a square of that color paper)
- space large enough to stand and move arms freely to the side and above yourself

Recipe Directions
1. Stand facing East. Hold your Athame in your output hand (hand you naturally point with) with your forefinger on the back of the blade, extending your arm straight out in front of you at shoulder height. Position the blade flat or parallel to the ground, cutting edge facing right.

2. Pull in the color you have chosen to use from the color source and extend a beam about 3 to 4 feet off the end of your blade. Beginners usually point their input hand towards the color source, pulling the energy with their intention from it into the hand, up the arm, across the shoulders, down the other arm and into the

Athame.

3. Holding your Athame very steady, turn in a clockwise circle (to the right), using the energy from your Athame to draw a horizontal circle all the way around you. Stop when you reach your starting point.

4. Now raise your arm straight into the air and point the tip of the Athame upward to draw your second circle (a vertical circle in front of you). Position your Athame so that the cutting edge leads all the way around the circle (overhead, right, down, left and overhead). You may have to adjust your hand position halfway through the circle to ensure that the cutting edge is leading. Be sure to do this carefully so that you do not cut yourself accidentally with the knife and make sure no one else is close enough to get in your way or get cut.

5. Keeping your Athame overhead, draw the final circle (a vertical circle beside you). Again, make sure that the cutting edge of your Athame is always leading. This orientation is the factor that causes the circles to spin so that you end up with a whirling shield rather than a static one.

6. Key your Fire omnil by seeing energies or experiences or problems that you want to key out shattering on the omnil, being deflected to the right or being bounced back to the sender. You can also key your own thoughts and energies out of the omnil by seeing yourself pushing them outside of it. Remember, if you don't key your omnil, it will keep everything out.

7. Unlike Air omnils, Fire omnils last indefinitely or until you cut them down. Like Air omnils, they get stronger when they are under attack. You can continue to key your Fire omnil at any time, even if it's

long after you put it up. If you start to feel isolated, take your omnil down – it means you've keyed it against too many things and it's starting to isolate you from your life.

8. To take down a Fire omnil:
    * Load your Athame with the same color as your omnil.
    * Extend a beam off the tip of your Athame that is slightly longer than the beam you used to create the omnil.
    * Cut the last circle with an overhead chop from right to left.
    * Cut the first 2 circles with an overhead cut that starts slightly behind you and goes past the horizontal plane in front of you.

How to Use the Results of Your Recipe

The color you use to build your ommil depends on what purpose you are building it for. This list will help you decide which color to use:

* **Sun Yellow:** Life Energy. Vitalizes the Spirit and can be used by the Spirit for any purpose.
* **Yellow Orange:** Vitalizes the Spirit and energizes the physical neural system. Too much of this color can produce nerve damage and burn out. It is also the color of anxiety or nervousness. This color omnil will also attract attention so put one on if you want to be the "life of the party", then remember to take it down after the party.
* **Red Orange:** Energizes the physical neural system and the body metabolism. Too much of this color produces high fever, can produce nerve damage and is the color band associated with pain, anger, and hostility.
* **Bright Red:** Boost the body's metabolism. Too much of this color produces high temperature. This color omnil can be used to deflect or maintain heat.

- **Red Purple:** Liquid heat. This color affects the temperature and flow of fluids in the glands, circulatory system, liver, kidneys, heart and other organs. Too much of this color can cause blood clots, glandular disorders or swelling.
- **Electric Blue:** Used mainly for shielding, religious invocations, conjurations and banishments. This color is a bridge between physical, psychic, and spiritual levels. Too much of this color, especially in a burst or a bolt, severely stuns a spirit. This is the energy band of radioactivity, and all radio waves travel in this band. It is the color you see in the blue part of a flame. This color omnil is often used for protection and by keying an electric blue omnil against electric blue, it will be programmed to defend against psychic attack.

Chalice: Four Element House Cleaning

The Firebowl covers the elements Air and Fire, and the Chalice covers the elements Water and Earth (notice how they relate to the charge verses for each tool). You can four element cleanse your home, other people and objects. The four element cleansing is just like the two element cleansing with the addition of Water and Earth.

Ingredients
- charged Firebowl
- charged Chalice
- spring water
- sea salt
- charcoal disk
- wood shavings
- pine resin
- ground sage
- wooden or paper matches
- sun candle

Recipe Directions

1. Charge your Firebowl and your Chalice using the recipe *"Charging Firebowl and Chalice"*.

2. Follow the directions above for doing the two element house cleaning with the Firebowl.

3. Now that you are back to the place you started with the Firebowl, pick up your charged Chalice.

4. To cleanse with your Chalice, dip two fingers into the water and flick them against your thumb to flick the water on the wall (about chest high). Start in the same place as you did with the Firebowl, flicking the water over the same spot where you put your first Lemniscate.

5. Follow the same directions as you did going along the walls with the Firebowl. Spritz water on the walls, doors, shelves, etc. every 2 to 3 feet until you return to your starting point. Keep spritzing until you are 3 to 5 feet past your starting point to complete the cleansing.

6. If you need to add water to your Chalice, you can add it without recharging the Chalice.

7. If you have any water left after you have completed the cleansing, you can wait until dark and pour it down the drain. You might see a blue glow around the drain for a minute or so after you pour the water. The water will also help to clean the pipes.

How to Use the Results of Your Recipe

A Four Element Cleansing is good for removing psychic imprints from walls, objects, and people. It can clear out negative energies or influences and any psychic residue left by any type of beings. We all encounter negative energies daily, so taking the time to clear these energies out of your living space will add to your peace of mind and being.

Pantacle(Plate): Come Alongs

Come Alongs are a magickal technique to help you attract what you want to bring into your life. They are not quite as powerful as a candle spell but are a good way for those who don't have much magickal background to get started.

Ingredients

- a keyed plate (see *"Cleansing and Keying Tools"* recipe)
- a magnet or Sun Yellow candle
- paper
- pen or pencil

Recipe Directions

1. Before beginning the actual Come Along, you will need to write a set of Directors and Limiters on a piece of paper. This is a very important step, as it will define very clearly what you want to have happen and what you do not want to have happen. Your Directors will be a very clear description as to specifically what you want. Do not go into how you want it to happen as that is the Universe's part, just stick to specifically what you do want. For example, don't just say "I want money", instead say something more like, "I want $1000.00 within the next 3-4 months". Then write your Limiters which is a list of things you do not want to have happen for you to get that money. For example, you might say "I want this money to come from totally legal means and not as the result of the death or harm to another person or by damage to or loss of property."

2. Now that you have a written list of Directors and Limiters, place them on your keyed Plate.

3. You can now choose to use either a Sun Yellow candle or a magnet for this step.

- Charge the candle with the verse:
  "Child of wonder, child of flame
  Nourish my Spirit and bring my aim!"
  Then place the candle on top of your written list on your Plate and leave it burning for about an hour. According to the amount of force and energy you need for what you are trying to attract, you may need to relight and charge the candle much more than just one time. Be sure to use fire safety precautions while the candle is burning so that it does not ignite the paper or anything else.

- Using a magnet is another way to do this step. If you cannot be in the area to keep an eye on your lit candle, then this may be a preferable method. You can also leave it set up on your Plate and not have to do multiple sessions. Simply place a large magnet on top of the list on your keyed Plate to draw what you have specified on paper to you.

How to Use the Results of Your Recipe

If you are somewhere that you do not have your keyed Plate, you can do a quick key method on any type of plate to perform a Come Along. Place your hands on either side of the Plate. Grip it with your thumbs on the top surface and the rest of your fingers supporting the underside of it. Look at a Grass Green Earth energy color source and begin flowing Grass Green energy from your dominant hand (hand you naturally point with) through the Plate into your other hand. Keep the energy flowing up your arm, across your shoulders, down the arm of your dominant hand and out your output hand again. Circulate Grass Green for about three minutes, then pull your Earth energy back into your body. You will know the Plate is keyed when it feels slightly tingly, heavy, warm, or loaded or definitely different than before you keyed it in some way.

[this page intentionally left blank]

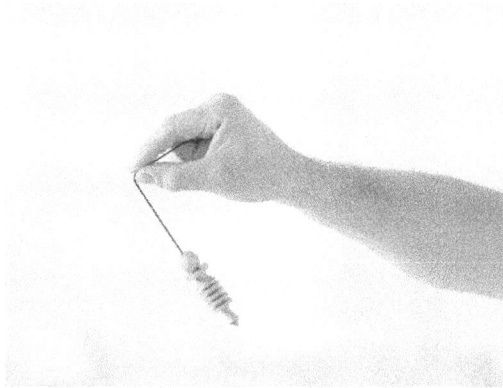

Tools of Magick Dessert Recipes

Desserts: Making Magick from Everyday Objects

Toolkit Using Everyday Objects

Uses for Everyday Tools

"Real magick is the ability to take a paperclip and transform it into a pendulum. Or shrink a problem by using an apple. Or turn an ordinary rock into a tool to unload problems. How magickal is that?"
~ Hana B., Fayetteville, GA

[this page intentionally left blank]

Create a Psychic Magick Talisman

"Shamanism is about shape shifting. Shamanism is about doing phenomenology with a tool kit that works."
~ Terence McKenna

Time Required: Thirty Minutes

Have you ever wished that you could carry your magickal tools with you wherever you go? While that would be nice, most people feel that carrying around a large Athame or even a long Wand to be a tad awkward. And if you are traveling by plane, airport security is certainly not going to allow you to bring a knife of any size on the plane. With a little creative thinking and ingenuity however, you can make your own traveling magickal toolkit with ordinary objects or just use ordinary objects that you find wherever you are as magickal tools. Any ordinary object that fits the requirements for the magickal tool you want to use it as, that is properly cleansed and is keyed for your personal use, can be used in the same way as a magickal tool. Here are some examples to get you started thinking what you have or can easily find wherever you are to substitute for magickal tools.

Ingredients

- Items you find in the environment you find yourself in or within your own home or find in secondhand stores.

Recipe Directions

1. Gather items ahead of time to take with you on your travels or keep in your purse or car or if you find yourself somewhere that you don't have your tools and need them, look around to see what might meet the criteria for a certain tool. For example:
   - Firebowl – flowerpot, kitchen bowl, wide vase.
   - Wand – small piece of ironwood, small piece of polished coral.
   - Athame – kitchen knife, hunting knife, pie spatula.
   - Chalice – goblet, wine glass, small silver doll size glass with stem.
   - Pantacle – kitchen plate, round tray, glass, or ceramic coaster.

2. Other ordinary objects can be used as magickal tools if properly cleansed and keyed. For example, a talisman or amulet can be keyed to your own energies for protection or providing certain types of characteristics or energies that you wish to have at your disposal. For example, if you are a serious type of person and would like to be more joyful or "lighten up" and laugh more, you might find a pendant of a hummingbird or a bracelet with a coyote on it as these are characteristics these totem animals can bring to you. When you find your item, you will need to key it in this manner:
   - Put the object in your dominant hand (usually the hand with which you point or write)

- Hold the object and flow energy into it. If you want to use the tool for a specific purpose, flow images or thoughts about that purpose through your hand as well. You can also chant a spell verse while doing this if appropriate.

- Continue with this process until the magick tool feels "charged," warm, or tingly. At that point, your magick tool has been keyed to your specific energy and will work for you personally.

3. There are also ways to do emergency keying on your everyday tools if you do not have the time or materials to do a full keying.
   - **Wand**
   o The object you are substituting for a Wand will need to be keyed using a Firebowl as described in the Wand section of the "Keying Magickal Tools" recipe.
   o You can use a makeshift Firebowl out of a bowl or vase or flowerpot filled with sand and find some sage in the kitchen and some pine needles to burn in it.
   o Then follow the directions given previously for keying the Wand.
   - **Athame**
   o Point the tip of the knife (or object that you are making into an Athame) to the North.
   o Strike the butt of the handle forcefully with anything hard, such as an iron skillet, a stone, or a hammer.
   o Your makeshift Athame will stay keyed for 15 minutes to one day by this method.
   - **Chalice**
   o Cup your hands on either side of the bowl of the Chalice.
   o Using a Water Blue color source, begin circling Water Blue from your output hand through the

Chalice into your input hand, up your input arm, across your shoulders, down your output arm and out your output hand again.

o Circulate Water Blue for about 3 minutes, then pull your water energy back in and you will have a temporarily keyed Chalice.

- **Plate**
o Place your hands on either side of the Plate.
o Grip the Plate with your thumbs on the top surface of the Plate and the rest of your fingers supporting the underside of the Plate.
o Look at a Grass Green Earth energy color source and begin flowing Grass Green energy from your dominant hand (hand you naturally point with) through the Plate into your other hand.
o Keep the energy flowing up your arm, across your shoulders, down the arm of your dominant hand and out your output hand again.
o Circulate Grass Green for about three minutes, then pull your Earth energy back into your body.
o You will know the Plate is keyed when it feels slightly tingly, heavy, warm, or loaded or different than before you keyed it in some way.

How to Use the Results of Your Recipe

You will need to cleanse, key, and store your everyday tools in the same manner as described earlier in this eBook for each tool. For instances when you need a Firebowl, you can use one you have made from a flowerpot, filled with some sand, and burning sage and pine resin on it and for those that require a Chalice you can use a wine glass Chalice filled with spring water and salt to make cleaning and keying very doable. When looking for substitutions for tools, consider the shape and best materials for the tool, then look around where you are at and see what you have that meets that criterion the best. Or visit a nearby thrift store and you may be able to find things there that will fit the bill. You might want to gather items ahead of time for traveling, wrap them in cotton such as a cotton bandana or scarf and put in a pouch so that you have your own magickal toolkit to take with you that will pass through any security without trouble.

[this page intentionally left blank]

Uses for Everyday Tools

*"When you really consider the everyday things around you,
they start to seem like tiny miracles."*
~ Amy Shearn

Time Required: Thirty Minutes

This recipe will give you a few ideas on how to use everyday objects as magickal tools in practical ways.

Ingredients

- paper clip or small stone
- string
- apple
- keyed Plate
- paper and pen or pencil
- bag or sack
- several palm sized or smaller rocks
- place to walk that has rocks and a large body of water

Recipe Directions

1. Pendulum unwind
   - Make a pendulum by tying a paper clip or small stone on the end of a string.

   - First cleanse your pendulum with smoke. The smoke from burning pine resin and sage works well. Just hold the pendulum over a column of smoke from your Firebowl until the smoke begins to "stick" to it.

   - Next, your pendulum needs to be keyed so that it responds to your energies. To key it, hold your pendulum in your dominant hand (the hand you write or point with). Flow energy into the pendulum for a minute or two, or until it grows warm and tingly.

   - Begin training your pendulum by establishing its yes and no directions. Decide if you want your pendulum to indicate "yes" with a vertical or horizontal swing. The "no" indicator will be the opposite of the "yes" indicator (if "yes" is a vertical swing, then "no" is a horizontal swing). Hold your pendulum suspended from your dominant hand. Rest your elbow on a table or your knee to stabilize your hand and swing your pendulum in a gentle clockwise circle telling it, "Show me yes." Wait for the pendulum to settle into the proper swing (whatever direction you chose). If it doesn't, ask again. Once your pendulum consistently swings in the proper direction for "yes," use the same process to ask it to show you the proper swing for "no."

   - Now you are ready to start training your pendulum to give you actual answers by practicing asking questions about short futures. Ask yes/no questions that can be verified in a 15 to 30 minute time frame. For instance, at the end of the work day you might ask your pendulum, "Will my roommate be home in the next 20 minutes?" Verify the correctness of your pendulum's answer, and then ask another question. In the beginning, it doesn't matter whether your pendulum gives you the correct answer or not, this is just the practice period and giving your pendulum a lot of practice is the important thing right now. The more you work with your pendulum, the more accurate it will become. Don't get obsessed with the "rightness" of the answers during this training period.

- Once you are getting reliable results from the training phase of using your pendulum, you can use it to help clear problems or issues that you are struggling with in your life. Start by holding your pendulum in your dominant hand, letting it dangle while you visualize the problem you want to clear.

- Ask your pendulum, "Can I, May I, Should I, clear this situation?" If you get a yes answer from your pendulum, then move forward. This is an important step because sometimes there is a life lesson to be learned from a specific problem you are facing that should not be interfered with. If the answer is no, stop this procedure.

- If you have determined it is okay to clear the problem, begin swinging your pendulum in a counter clockwise direction, asking it to clear the situation. As you do this, "see" the situation resolving in your mind. Be very specific with your request and what you envision as to the situation being resolved – not how but what it would look like to not have the problem.

- Continue to focus on clearing the situation until your pendulum stops spinning in the counter clockwise direction. It will then either start moving along a vertical or horizontal axis, stop or start spinning clockwise. When it stops swinging on its own then the problem has been cleared.

- Once a problem has been cleared you can of course always choose to bring it back if you really want to, but instead try trusting the power of your pendulum and your intent and release the problem from your consciousness. If you find it creeping back into your consciousness throughout the day, change your focus to something else. This is a good procedure to use on clearing out repetitive thoughts that you find yourself having, especially in the case of negative thoughts which you want to clear out to avoid attracting those negative situations to you. Instead of visualizing a situation you want resolved just hold the repetitive thought in your mind and ask your pendulum to clear the thought from your life. After the process, you may still find the thought popping up in your mind occasionally, but it should appear far less frequently than before and eventually will disappear.

2. Shrink problems away
   - This technique works well for things you want to shrink away from your life using a plain, ordinary apple. Examples would be your level of body fat or a chronic bad habit that you can't seem to shake.

   - If you are looking to shrink something that is of a more complicated nature, you may need a list of Directors and Limiters written out on a piece of paper. (see description in recipe *"Using Magick Tools"* under the *"Come Alongs"* section with using the Plate)

- If you use Directors and Limiters, fold the list and place it on your keyed Plate.

- Key the apple to the problem or situation that you want to reduce by holding the apple in your dominant hand while you think about everything you can about the situation. Using your intention, focus on all the details about the situation and the information you wrote about it in your Directors and Limiters. You can flow thoughts and/or emotions about the situation into the apple. The more details you use, the more accurately the apple will be keyed to your situation.

- When the apple feels charged, full, warm, heavy, tingly, or different in a magickal or energetic sense then it is keyed and ready to use. Put it on top of your keyed Plate on top of the folded list of Directors and Limiters.

- If you quick keyed your Plate instead of using a more permanent keying method, you will need to quick key it each day for your Plate to stay keyed. This also gives you a chance to restate your intentions which helps the procedure along. You can strengthen the procedure by re-keying the plate daily and then reading your Directors and Limiters aloud while holding the apple in your dominant hand. This adds energy to the relationship between the situation and the apple.

- Now here comes the hardest part for some people – Wait and be Patient! The goal is to achieve a permanent and lasting result and that takes time, energy and daily maintenance. This procedure can take from several weeks to several months to manifest. Negative energy like impatience will only hinder it, so be sure to stay in a positive mood especially when doing your daily keying.

- Over time your apple will wither and with it the situation you keyed to be represented by the apple will wither with it. Be sure that you are keying the apple to be a situation or issue and NOT a person or other living thing. If a person is causing your problem, this is NOT the technique to deal with them as causing harm to another being is against the Rules of the Road that govern magickal practice.

3. Toss away troubles
    - This magic technique uses simulacra magick using rocks to represent problems or negative issues you are facing. In simulacra magic, an object is keyed to represent a person or thing and then whatever is done to the simulacra also happens to the person or thing it is keyed to. In this procedure you will be creating a psychic connection between a rock and a problem in your life and then throwing the rock in a body of water to toss it away. Be sure you are dealing with issues, behaviors, or situations and NOT people or other living things as being the source of your trouble. Bringing harm to another living being is against the Rules of the Road that govern magickal practice.

    - Pick a place to go for a walk that has some type of rocks or stones and has a large body of water such as a lake, pond or river and take a sack or bag with you.

    - As you begin walking look for rocks that call to you in some way and pick up one that draws your attention and that will be easy enough to put in your sack.

- Hold the rock in your dominant hand, the hand that you naturally point with, and think of the problem that you want to key to this rock.

- Key the rock by holding it in your dominant hand, and bringing up every thought, feeling, or physical sensation related to the problem or issue you have. Push all these with intention into the rock. Be sure that you are NOT keying the rock to a living person or being, but only the situation or problem that you are facing.

- Once the stone gets an energetically heavy feeling to it, becomes warm or tingly, you will know it is keyed and can place it in your sack.

- Continue your walk doing the same with other rocks and other problems until you feel you have a rock for each of the problems or issues you want to deal with.

- Now take your sack of rocks to the body of water and take one stone out of the sack. Hold the stone for a few seconds then toss it with all your might into the water. This physical disconnection will sever the issue from your life.

- You can also say the following disconnect litany in a voice of command just before throwing the rock into the water if you wish.
"I am neither your creature nor your get,
To be moved by your whim or your let;
I will go my own way,
By night or by day,
To serve my own purposes yet."

- Continue throwing the rocks in this way one by one into the water and once your sack is empty you are done.

- This will disconnect you from the problems that you opted to deal with. You can of course always choose to bring them back into your space, so just know that you have let them go and dwell on them no more. Find a way to distract yourself if you find that you are starting to wonder about them again.

How to Use the Results of Your Recipe

Using these examples, you will be able to find similar uses that suit your individual need or problem. Just be sure you stay on the right side of the Rules of the Road (presented at the front of this ebook) that govern magickal practice and especially before performing any act of magick, Take Your Time and Think it Through.

More Magickal Resources

Kindle or Paperback on Amazon:
1. *Witchcraft Spell Book Series:*
   - Learn How to Do Witchcraft Rituals and Spells with Your Bare Hands (Witchcraft Spell Books, Book 1)
   - Learn How to Do Witchcraft Rituals and Spells with Household Ingredients (Witchcraft Spell Books, Book 2)
   - Learn How to Do Witchcraft Rituals and Spells with Magical Tools (Witchcraft Spell Books, Book 3)
   - Witchcraft Spell Book: The Complete Guide of Witchcraft Rituals & Spells for Beginners (compilation of Books 1, 2, & 3)
2. *Kitchen Table Magick Series*

Ebooks and Online Courses at *www.shamanschool.com*
   - Wand: Air Tool
   - Athame: Fire Tool
   - Chalice: Water Tool
   - Plate: Earth Tool
   - Magical Tool: Firebowl
   - Psychic Development
   - Energy Healing For Self and Others

- How to Do Voodoo
- Daily Rituals to Attract What You Want in Life

Find a complete list of magickal resources on https://amzn.to/3swxvPo. These resources are constantly updated so check back often!

Free Gift Offer

To thank you for purchasing this book, I'd like to give you a

100% FREE GIFT

Learn more about your free magickal gift.

Access Your Free Gift at www.shamanschool.com

Find a complete list of magickal resources on https://amzn.to/3swxvPo. These resources are constantly updated so check back often!

About G. Alan Joel

Magick means many things to different people. The form of magick taught by G. Alan Joel for more than 30 years is steeped in tribal traditions from around the world, from both modern tribal cultures and those from the past, which have been mostly passed on through oral dialog.

At the very heart of the magick that Mr. Joel teaches is the use of Universal Laws for the benefit of self, others, and even the planet. These magickal traditions can take on many forms, including simple rituals for daily use, specific spells for particular life situations, the use of simulacra (often better known as voodoo), weather working, water witching, the use of the elemental tools (Firebowl, Wand, Athame, Chalice, and Plate), magickal self-defense rituals, and more. Also included are the use of the Tarot for divination and spellwork, divination rituals of all kinds, Spirit-to-Spirit communication, exercises for psychic development, and abundant healing techniques.

Through his 30 plus years of studying, teaching, and honing his magickal practice, G. Alan Joel has helped thousands of people successfully integrate the magickal, and seemingly miraculous, into their daily lives. In fact, one of the greatest gifts Mr. Joel has offered through his teachings is the ability for his students to always find a magickal solution for life situations that often seem impossible to solve. With magick, anything is possible in the mundane world. All that is required of the practitioner is an open mind, the desire to learn, and a willingness to pay some time and effort into his or her magickal practice. One of Mr. Joel's favorite quotes is:

"What you pay into your practice pays you back!"

While many magickal traditions have fiercely guarded their secrets from the public, Mr. Joel feels that "Magick is the birthright of every planetary citizen." As such he strives to offer magickal teachings that are easily learned and inexpensive (no excessive fees to join exclusive magickal groups or ascend up the levels of learning). He also offers techniques that are usable and effective for all who are sincere in their desire to practice magick. In essence, Mr. Joel's methods teach a form of "Every Man's (and Woman's) Magick." All are welcome, his teachings are simple yet effective, and he also offers online classes in which he helps students troubleshoot their magickal issues in an interactive setting.

Find out more about Mr. Joel's teachings here and on his website (***www.shamanschool.com***) where magickal offerings are updated on a regular basis.

Mr. Joel augments this magickal knowledge and teaching with 30 years of practice as Doctor of Chinese Medicine, including a deep understanding of herbology and acupuncture. His understanding of the healing arts deepens the magickal knowledge he teaches, as magickal healing is a major aspect of his teachings. Mr. Joel believes that while there is clearly a time and place for Western Medicine, magickal and Eastern healing techniques can be harmoniously blended in to offer people many choices for healing all types of health conditions.

About the Esoteric School of Shamanism and Magic

The Esoteric School of Shamanism and Magic was started from a desire for all people from all over the globe to be able to attend a real, if virtual, school dedicated to magick and shamanism. The aim of the Esoteric School of Shamanism and Magic is to help people create permanent, positive change in their lives through the study of esoteric magickal and shamanic knowledge. It doesn't matter what your esoteric background is, whether you started out with witchcraft, religious studies, spirituality or candle magick, we welcome you. We believe that the Truth is the same, no matter which form you practice. We delight in all manner of shamanic schools and traditions, magickal techniques and esoteric ritual. You can visit us at ***www.shamanschool.com***, our blog at ***http://shamanmagic.blogspot.com***, or on social media via links on our website.

[this page intentionally left blank]

[this page intentionally left blank]

[this page intentionally left blank]

[this page intentionally left blank]

www.ingramcontent.com/pod-product-compliance
Lightning Source LLC
Chambersburg PA
CBHW071906020426
42331CB00010B/2689